House OF Lisabeth Design Magazine

I0419191

May 2015 Issue

Evolution may explain why men like curvy bottoms see more on page 5.......

Design & Concepts L.L.C
March 2015 Issue

House of:
Lisabeth Design
Magazine

Today's Issue:

- *Doggy's world*
- *Fashion No's*
- *Design or Not*
- *Featured Business*

House of Lisabeth Design Magazine 2015

Evolution May Explain Why Men Like Curvy Bottoms

These curvaceous gals would have had an evolutionary advantage, in that they appeared able to bear multiple children easily, the researchers said.

"This spinal structure would have enabled pregnant women to balance their weight over the hips," said study leader David Lewis, a UT Austin alumnus and now a psychologist at Bilkent University in Turkey.

"These women would have been more effective at foraging during pregnancy and less likely to suffer spinal injuries," he said in a UT Austin news release. "In turn, men who preferred these women would have had mates who were better able to provide for fetus and offspring, and who would have been able to carry out multiple pregnancies without injury."

This preference evolved over thousands of years and is likely to persist for a long time, the researchers noted.

Their conclusions came from a two-part study in which 100 men were asked to look at images of women and rate their attractiveness. Women with a 45.5-degree in the lower back were rated as most appealing. The researchers next determined from a group of 200 men that guys preferred this degree of lower back curvature regardless of a woman's butt size.

"What's fascinating about this research is that it is yet another scientific illustration of a close fit between a sex-differentiated feature of human morphology -- in this case lumbar curvature -- and an evolved standard of attractiveness," study co-author David Buss, a UT Austin psychology professor, said in the news release.

"This adds to a growing body of evidence that beauty is not entirely arbitrary, or 'in the eyes of the beholder' as many in mainstream social science believed, but rather has a coherent adaptive logic," he said.

The study was published online March 19 in the journal Evolution and Human Behavior.

Opinions Section: Dating online

Every day, millions of single adults, worldwide, visit an online dating site. Many are lucky, finding life-long love or at least some exciting escapades. Others are not so lucky. The industry—eHarmony, Match, OkCupid, and a thousand other online dating sites—wants singles and the general public to believe that seeking a partner through their site is not just an alternative way to traditional venues for finding a partner, but a superior way. Is it?

With our colleagues Paul Eastwick, Benjamin Karney, and Harry Reis, we recently published a book-length article in the journal Psychological Science in the Public Interest that examines this question and evaluates online dating from a scientific perspective. One of our conclusions is that the advent and popularity of online dating are terrific developments for singles, especially insofar as they allow singles to meet potential partners they otherwise wouldn't have met. We also conclude, however, that online dating is not better than conventional offline dating in most respects, and that it is worse is some respects.

Beginning with online dating's strengths: As the stigma of dating online has diminished over the past 15 years, increasing numbers of singles have met romantic partners online. Indeed, in the U.S., about 1 in 5 new relationships begins online. Of course, many of the people in these relationships would have met somebody offline, but some would still be single and searching. Indeed, the people who are most likely to benefit from online dating are precisely those who would find it difficult to meet others through more conventional methods, such as at work, through a hobby, or through a friend.

For example, online dating is especially helpful for people who have recently moved to a new city and lack an established friendship network, who possess a minority sexual orientation, or who are sufficiently committed to other activities, such as work or childrearing, that they can't find the time to attend events with other singles.

It's these strengths that make the online dating industry's weaknesses so disappointing. We'll focus on two of the major weaknesses here: the overdependence on profile browsing and the overheated emphasis on "matching algorithms."

Ever since Match.com launched in 1995, the industry has been built around profile browsing. Singles browse profiles when considering whether to join a given site, when considering whom to contact on the site, when turning back to the site after a bad date, and so forth. Always, always, it's the profile.

What's the problem with that, you might ask? Sure, profile browsing is imperfect, but can't singles get a pretty good sense of whether they'd be compatible with a potential partner based on that person's profile? The answer is simple: No, they cannot.

A series of studies spearheaded by our co-author Paul Eastwick has shown that people lack insight regarding which characteristics in a potential partner will inspire or undermine their attraction to him or her (see here, here, and here). As such, singles think they're making sensible decisions about who's compatible with them when they're browsing profiles, but they can't get an accurate sense of their romantic compatibility until they've met the person face-to-face (or perhaps via webcam; the jury is still out on richer forms of computer-mediated communication). Consequently, it's unlikely that singles will make better decisions if they browse profiles for 20 hours rather than 20 minutes.

The straightforward solution to this problem is for online dating sites to provide singles with the profiles of only a handful of potential partners rather than the hundreds or thousands of profiles that many sites provide. But how should dating sites limit the pool?

Here we arrive at the second major weakness of online dating: the available evidence suggests that the mathematical algorithms at matching sites are negligibly better than matching people at random (within basic demographic constraints, such as age, gender, and education). Ever since eHarmony.com, the first algorithm-based matching site, launched in 2000, sites such as Chemistry.com, PerfectMatch.com, GenePartner.com, and FindYourFaceMate.com have claimed that they have developed a sophisticated matching algorithm that can find singles a uniquely compatible mate.

These claims are not supported by any credible evidence. In our article, we extensively reviewed the procedures such sites use to build their algorithms, the (meager and unconvincing) evidence they have presented in support of their algorithm's accuracy, and whether the principles underlying the algorithms are sensible. To be sure, the exact details of the algorithm cannot be evaluated because the dating sites have not yet allowed their claims to be vetted by the scientific community (eHarmony, for example, likes to talk about its "secret sauce"), but much information relevant to the algorithms is in the public domain, even if the algorithms themselves are not.

From a scientific perspective, there are two problems with matching sites' claims. The first is that those very sites that tout their scientific bona fides have failed to provide a shred of evidence that would convince anybody with scientific training. The second is that the weight of the scientific evidence suggests that the principles underlying current mathematical matching algorithms—similarity and complementarity—cannot achieve any notable level of success in fostering long-term romantic compatibility.

It is not difficult to convince people unfamiliar with the scientific literature that a given person will, all else equal, be happier in a long-term relationship with a partner who is similar rather than dissimilar to them in terms of personality and values. Nor is it difficult to convince such people that opposites attract in certain crucial ways.

The problem is that relationship scientists have been investigating links between similarity, "complementarity" (opposite qualities), and marital well-being for the better part of a century, and little evidence supports the view that either of these principles—at least when assessed by characteristics that can be measured in surveys—predicts marital well-being. Indeed, a major meta-analytic review of the literature by Matthew Montoya and colleagues in 2008 demonstrates that the principles have virtually no impact on relationship quality. Similarly, a 23,000-person study by Portia Dyrenforth and colleagues in 2010 demonstrates that such principles account for approximately 0.5 percent of person-to-person differences in relationship well-being.

To be sure, relationship scientists have discovered a great deal about what makes some relationships more successful than others. For example, such scholars frequently videotape couples while the two partners discuss certain topics in their marriage, such as a recent conflict or important personal goals. Such scholars also frequently examine the impact of life circumstances, such as unemployment stress, infertility problems, a cancer diagnosis, or an attractive co-worker. Scientists can use such information about people's interpersonal dynamics or their life circumstances to predict their long-term relationship well-being.

But algorithmic-matching sites exclude all such information from the algorithm because the only information those sites collect is based on individuals who have never encountered their potential partners (making it impossible to know how two possible partners interact) and who provide very little information relevant to their future life stresses (employment stability, drug abuse history, and the like).

So the question is this: Can online dating sites predict long-term relationship success based exclusively on information provided by individuals—without accounting for how two people interact or what their likely future life stressors will be? Well, if the question is whether such sites can determine which people are likely to be poor partners for almost anybody, then the answer is probably yes.

Read more at:

Sprecher, Susan. "The Scientific Flaws of Online Dating Sites." Scientific American Global RSS. N.p., 22 Apr. 2015. Web. 22 Apr. 2015.

DESIGN SEO STYLE CREATE SEO LIFE

The table at which I am sitting measures 75 centimetres by 90 centimetres, which, anywhere else, would be a table for four. At the new Kent Street Kitchen, however, it's a table for two. Everything here is big. It's like dining in the Land of the Giants. After a four-month renovation, the rooms that once housed The Observatory's formal 60-seater Galileo restaurant and Library Bar now form one long room the size of an auditorium, seating 140. Floral displays are enormous; chandeliers, gigantic.

That's what happens when a luxury hotel group such as The Langham moves to sunny Sydney. More accustomed to Hong Kong's high rents or London's tight squeeze on space, it's spreading its wings

The World of Entertainment

TOP PICKS OF THIS MONTH.....

Ask: The Counterintuitive Online Formula to Discover Exactly What Your Customers Want to Buy...Create a Mass of Raving Fans...and Take Any Business to the Next Level
 by Ryan Levesque

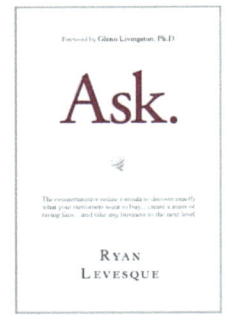

"What Ryan Levesque has done is give you the art and the science behind figuring out EXACTLY what your prospects want... and then delivering it via an incredibly effective sales process

Tsunami
 by Saddleback Educational Publishing Staff
Themes: Hi-Lo, Family life, adventure, travel. These traditional reads are brimming with spirited characters and positive values--but with a little extra excitement and bite, so hold on to your hats! Written expressly for the middle grade struggling reader, the series does not contain strong language, edgy themes, or dysfunctional families.

Creature
 by
 Saddleback Educational Publishing
Themes: Hi-Lo, Family life, adventure, travel. These traditional reads are brimming with spirited characters and positive values--but with a little extra excitement and bite, so hold on to your hats! Written expressly for the middle grade struggling reader, the series does not contain strong language, edgy themes, or dysfunctional families.

AccessVegas.com

Showroom - The Orleans Hotel
Las Vegas, NV
Saturday
4/25/2015

Le Rêve The Dream
Date: Monday 4/27/2015
 5 Day(s)
Time: 9:30 pm - 11:00 pm

Jobbing.com

Kenny Chesney with Jake Owen and Chas...
Tickets Now Available

Wednesday, April 29, 2015
@ Jobing.com Arena

April 26, 2015
Sunday   7:30 PM

Talking Stick Resort

9800 E Indian Bend road
Scottsdale, Arizona 85250

ENTERTAINMENT NIGHT LIFE

Check out these latest by: Joyce Keller

These are the hottest places we came about during our nights out....

Try a few martinis and a couple of nights here!

Las Vegas:

Chateau club
http://www.lasvegas.com/listing/paris-las-vegas/229/

VooDoo Rooftop Nightclub
http://www.lasvegas.com/listing/voodoo-rooftop-nightclub/6352/

Los Angelos:

Belasco Nightclub
http://funkytownla.com/

The Vault Night Club
http://www.thevaultnightclubla.com/

Phoenix, AZ

Q-Lounge
http://www.qloungephoenix.com/#upcoming-events

Cooperstown
http://www.alicecooperstown.com/

Fashion No or not….
Brought to you by: Lisabeths Design

Waxy Deep Green and Blue Ice Dress For Him Or Her

Green and blue have been the colors that illuminated the sea and our evening nights. A touch of sea weed and you might be in the middle of the Atlantic dancing away. Another touch would be a stunning blue eyed shade to a teal green to show that suttle clash.

You can check out Nordstroms were you have the all green collection for this spring. Anything from running shoes to the wedge classic, to the hill its all green. To find out how its trending we loked up varietys of waxy dress with blue and teal. Feathers are making a triumphant return to the runway in manners both bold and subdued. Erdem went all out in a waxy deep green and blue plumbed dress that was all drama – while Simone Rocha was sublte with airy wisps of feathers on the ends of her jackets.

Get the look in our Bae Boutique Wishes dress which in ivory and gold which is also coming soon as part of our new "Black Label" collection in black.

So lets plan on an sea like spring /summer with the blue and teal mermaids of the fashion world. And for the guys a simple bow will go......

Trendy News What You Want To Know

Gwyenth Paltro files divorce from Chris Martin
Paltrow cited irreconcilable differences in the documents, which were filed in Los Angeles on Monday after 11 years of marriage.
The papers request joint custody of their two children, Apple and Moses.
Paltrow, 42, and Martin, 38, announced their separation in March 2014, describing it as a "conscious uncoupling".

The actress's lifestyle blog Goop.com crashed after the couple posted a statement about their decision.

Trendy News What You Want To Know

People Names Sandra Bullock the World's Most Beautiful Woman!

Besides her striking beauty, Sandra, 50, has already had an amazing year to back up the magazine's honor. The actress can be heard voicing a supervillain in the upcoming movie Minions, which hits theaters on July 10. She also recently wrapped filming Our Brand Is Crisis

Trendy News What You Want To Know

Former 7th Heaven Star Passes away
TV and movie actress Sarah Goldberg, best known for playing Sarah Glass Camden on TV drama "7th Heaven," as well as roles in "House," "Judging Amy" and "Jurassic Park III," died of natural causes in her family's Wisconsin home on September 27 at the age of 40.

According to the Chicago Sun-Times, an autopsy was performed, but was unable to determine a specific cause of death. The actresses' mother, Judy, said that a heart ailment may have been the culprit. "She went to sleep and didn't wake up," her mother told the paper.

-

-

Trendy News What You Want To Know

Harry Styles' Old Tattoos Reveal A Major Clue About His Mysterious New Thigh Ink
This week, the most critical and urgent matter for One Direction fans isn't the misery of the band's first group photo or the progress of their new songs. It's what in the world Harry Styles' perplexing new tattoo might be.

more: Harry Styles Revealed A Mysterious New Tattoo In A Pic Of Chelsea Handler's Butt

In a totally random and baffling debut, the 21-year-old's new ink was spotted in a pic uploaded by Chelsea Handler on Saturday (April 18). The good news is, it's prominently placed on Harry's thigh, legitimizing our tendency to stare longingly at his legs. The bad news is, this is the only photo we have of it so far and it's still totally unclear what the tat actually is.

Workout Time: Best Exercises For Her and For Him: Part One

To me, exercises are unisex. But men and women have a different musculature and muscle-to-fat ratio, which definitely makes some moves more important to include your routine based on your gender.

Big chest, toned butt

Men have more muscle mass, less body fat and a broader shoulder to hip ratio than women. That's why we see men jump right into the chest press and women on any sitting leg machines such as leg extensions and hip abductors.

Here's what happens with these tendencies: Some men have big chest with "chicken legs" and some women have great legs but worry about the "folds" on the upper back and jiggly arms.

To get more of balanced body, I suggest adding to your routine two exercises (one for men and one for women) that will work those areas that need to catch up.

Credits: photos by Andrew Meade Photography, Inc., clothing by Lululemon Athletica, location Canyon Ranch Hotel & Spa Miami Beach

a) For Her:

Replace the leg machines with the Bulgarian. Single leg squat. This exercise taxes the legs like no others. It works the quadriceps, hamstring and butt all in one; plus the core. It can be performed with barbell or dumbbells. Some things to consider: a) the height of the bench should be knee high, b) the farther the rear leg sits, the more that the gluteus works. It's important that you sit back while reaching a 90 degree angle with the working leg. Advanced: Bend over at the waist and with the dumbbells try to touch the floor by where the front foot is. This will engage more the gluteus and lower back. Perform this exercise in your leg workout for three to four sets of 10-12 reps.

For the upper back and triceps (back of the arms), do the straight arm lat pull down. This exercise will work the back muscles and the triceps at the same time. In particular, the teres major and latissimus dorsi muscles, which attachment to where the axial area is. Keep your arms straight over the bar and bring it down to your top of the thighs where your hands naturally rest. Make sure that you squeeze the scapula together, keep the chest up and don't shrug the shoulders and brace the core. Perform this exercise in your upper body workout for two to three sets of 12-15 reps.

CHECKOUT MORE AT THIS WEBSITE: http://martamontenegro.com/2011/07/best-exercises-for-her-or-him-part-one/

Trendy News What You Want To Know

Kourtney Kardashian Posts Flashback Photo of First Night She Met Scott Disick

Getting sentimental! Kourtney Kardashian posted a cute throwback photo of when she first met longtime love Scott Disick on Friday, Mar. 27.

PHOTOS: How star couples first met
"#FBF The night I met @letthelordbewithyou," she captioned the photo. The Keeping Up With the Kardashians star, now 35, sipped on a glass of wine and wore a chic summer dress in the pic. Disick, sitting on the opposite side of the couch, wore a black top and shorts.
Read more: http://www.usmagazine.com/celebrity-news/news/kourtney-kar dashian-posts-flashback-pic-of-night-she-met-scott-disick-2015283#ixzz3ViAsQVFd
Follow us: @usweekly on Twitter | usweekly on Facebook

 Diesel Gets Teased for Furious 7 Oscars Talk on Conan: Watch!
Read more: http://www.usmagazine.com/entertainment/news/vin-diesL-gets-teased-for-furious-7-oscars-talk-on-conan-

Vin Diesel said something interesting. In an interview, [he] said that Fast and Furious 7 will win the Oscar for Best Picture," the redhead host said. He cracked: "He's being kept in a hospital overnight for observation."

Trendy News What You Want To Know

Is this goodbye, Dr. Zoe Hart? Word is still out on whether Hart of Dixie's fourth season finale on Friday, Mar. 27 is in fact its last episode, but the show wrapped up perfectly if that's the case. Rachel Bilson's long-running CW series left fans with two weddings, one birth, and a huge musical number. (Only in Bluebell, Alabama!)

Read more: http://www.usmagazine.com/entertainment/news/hart-of-dixie-finale-two-weddings-one-baby-and-one-big-sing-along-2015283#ixzz3ViEX6sYe
Follow us: @usweekly on Twitter | usweekly on Facebook

The Celebrity Dumbing Down of Protest Culture
Two anniversaries this spring show how well-meaning but self-indulgent celebrities helped water down a great American tradition.

This month, two anniversaries seem to harmonize with one another. Fifty years ago, civil-rights protestors marching from Selma to Montgomery were rallying and singing and sometimes bleeding and dying for freedom. And 30 years ago, a feel-good anthem sung by rock stars to fight African hunger was climbing the charts. Moving from "We Shall Overcome" in 1965 to "We Are the World" in 1985 highlights African-Americans' miraculous leap forward in those two decades.

New Technology For The Modern Geek

iPhone 6s
At A Glance

Apple is expected to unveil its next-generation iPhones in the fall of 2015, and they may come with some impressive camera improvements.

Apple's iPhone 6 and 6 Plus, released in September, have only been available for a few months, but rumors about the next-generation iPhone are already trickling in. It's likely Apple will continue its 2014 trend, offering the 2015 iPhone in two separate sizes -- one larger and one smaller.

It's not clear what Apple will call its 2015 iPhones, but Apple may stick to its long running "S" naming scheme (which has been around since 2009), calling the new phones the iPhone 6s and the iPhone 6s Plus. iPhone 6s Plus is a mouthful though, so this might be the year that we get a new naming format.

We don't have many details on the next-generation iPhone yet, but because it's an "S" year and because the iPhone was just redesigned, it's likely the update will focus on internal improvements rather than a new external look. There may be at least one external change, though. There's been a rumor that Apple could add a new color option to its iPhone lineup in 2015 -- pink.

-

New Technology For The Modern Geek

Fujifilm Instax Mini 8 Instant Film Camera (White)
New slimmer and lighter body

• Automatic exposure measurement. The camera signals the recommended aperture setting with a flashing LED. This helps capture the perfect photo every time.

• New High-Key mode - Take brighter pictures with a soft look - perfect for portraits.

• New improved viewfinder for greater clarity and visibility.

-

New Technology For The Modern Geek

Elgato Smart Key(10027500)
Connect your key to your iPhone

• Get notifications whenever you leave your key behind
• Remember where your key was last seen
• Find your key by playing a sound
• Customize when, how and where you want to be notified

-

New Technology For The Modern Geek

Brookstone 2.4GHz Wireless TV Headphones

-

Great sound without the wires!
• Hear every detail in your TV show, movie or music
• Listen for up to 10 hours on a single charge
• Features noise reduction and high-def audio with deep bass effect
• Soft-touch padded headphones

-

New Technology For The Modern Geek

GolfBuddy Voice GPS
Audio Distance Information (It tells you the distance)

• Pre-Loaded with 35.000+ courses worldwide
• 8 different spoken languages pre-loaded
• Distance to Front / Center / Back
• Shot Distance Measurement

–

New Technology For The Modern Geek

Orbotix Ollie for Android and iOS - Retail Packaging - White

iOS & Android compatible
• Apps: Driving & Programming
• Ollie will travel up to 6.3 m/s (20.6 f/s, 14 mph)

New Technology VS The Other Guy

<u>40 years of gadgets come out to play</u>
<u>Technology, even equipment that's long outdated and shunted aside,</u>
<u>can still strike an emotional chord.</u>

Just ask Kimon Keramidas, curator of "The Interface Experience," an exhibit that rounds up tech milestones from 40 years of personal computing for visitors to see and touch. He said almost everyone has a favorite item they make a beeline to and greet like an old friend.

"It's either 'Oh my God, it was so great!' or 'Oh my God, that was so hard to use,'" Keramidas said. "It's an emotional thing. People are connecting at more than just an intellectual level."

-

The show, which opens Friday at the Focus Gallery of the Bard Graduate Center in New York City, offers visitors a trip through history with what is essentially a gadgety greatest hits. On display are more than 25 different devices, as well as a wall of more than a hundred mobile phones (what Keramidas calls his cell phone "petting zoo") -- all of which can be touched and, in some cases, played with.

-

<u>"Most computers in museums sit in a corner behind a glass wall; they're not turned on, and you can't touch them," said Keramidas. "I wanted to stage things so people could experience them and watch each other working on the devices."</u>

The centerpieces of the exhibit are five particular technologies that serve as markers for major stages in the development of interfaces for personal computing: the Commodore 64 as the first computer for the masses, the Apple MacIntosh for the introduction of a graphical user interface and the mainstream debut of a mouse, the PalmPilot as the first competent mobile device, the Apple iPad for introducing the touchscreen in tablet form and the Microsoft Kinect for making

-

-

Social apps and more
Find us !

Home and Garden: The New Front Yard For Spring!

Home improvement and garden events

<u>GARDEN</u>

Boerner Botanical Gardens: Variety of classes and events held year-round. 9400 Boerner Drive, Hales Corners. (414) 525-5653; boernerbotanicalgardens.org.

? Milwaukee Bonsai Society Meeting. April 7.

? The Healing Garden Expo. April 11.

? Rose Society Meeting. April 14.

? Iris Society Meeting. April 16.

Burlington Garden Center: Gardening, planting and lawn care workshops and seminars; open year-round. 5205 Mormon Road, Burlington, (262) 763-2153; burlingtongardencenter.com.

? Spring Garden Moot. April 11.

? New Gardener Day. April 18.

? Lawn Care. April 25.

Be Creative Go Out And Design Something

Design fashion trends entertainment technology and home and garden.

**House of Lisabeth
Design Magazine**

Mail to: Unit 8438 PO
Box 6945
London W1A6US

Tell readers to mail this back for a catalog,
brochure, or price list.

NAME _____

ADDRESS _____

_____

_____

Politics And More

Disciples Of Christ Church Threatens A Boycott Over New Indiana Bill That Allows LGBT Discrimination

Though the Christian Church (Disciples of Christ) has made Indianapolis its headquarters for nearly a century, the denomination is considering pulling its next biennial convention out of Indiana over a new state law that allows businesses to turn away gay customers.

Gov. Mike Pence signed the Religious Freedom Restoration Act on Thursday (March 26), the day after receiving a letter from church leaders pleading with him to veto it and threatening to move their 2017 General Assembly outside the state.

Muslim Women React To Ayaan Hirsi Ali's Stance On Islam

Activist Ayaan Hirsi Ali has been extremely vocal in her critique of Islam. In her new book, Heretic: Why Islam Needs a Reformation Now, she details her issues with its teachings and even declares "Islam is not a religion of peace."

A panel of Muslim women discussed Hirsi Ali's stance in a HuffPost Live conversation on Monday.

Watch the clip above and the full HuffPost Live conversation about millennial Muslims here.

ISIS Ideology Is Not True To Islam, And These Imams Are Fighting Back

Using a twisted version of Islam, the militant group Islamic State, or ISIS, has pushed online campaigns to attract youth to its bloody crusade in Syria and Iraq. Now a group of British imams and scholars is looking to "reclaim the Internet" with a new magazine aimed at shifting the conversation and spreading a message of truth.

Haqiqah, meaning "the truth" or "the reality" in Arabic, is a digital magazine created by Islamic scholars with the purpose of educating young people about the realities of extremism, according to its backers at Imams Online. The goal, they say, is to "drown out" the voices perpetuating violence.

Politics Transformed

THE HIGH-TECH BATTLE FOR YOUR VOTE

Politics: The who and what of politics

Huge Earthquake Kills Hundreds In Nepal, Triggers Everest Avalanche
A 7.8 magnitude earthquake struck Nepal on Saturday, killing over a thousand people, causing an avalanche on Mount Everest and leaving a wake of destruction across the broader region.

In Nepal, at least 1,382 people were killed, according to Nepal's Home Ministry.

The earthquake, the worst to hit Nepal in over 80 years, also triggered a deadly avalanche on Mount Everest.

Allies Are Not Like Facebook Friends: US Should Drop Useless and Dangerous Alliances
If America ends up at war, it almost certainly will be on behalf of one ally or another. Washington collects allies like most people collect Facebook "friends." The vast majority of U.S. allies are security liabilities, tripwires for conflict and war.

Perhaps even worse, American officials constantly abase themselves, determined to reassure the very countries which the U.S. is defending at great cost and risk. Indeed, America's most hawkish politicians, who routinely posture like reincarnations of Winston Churchill, routinely talk of sacrificing U.S. lives, wealth, and security for the benefit of other nations. For instance, Sen. Marco Rubio (R-Fl.) recently worried, "What ally around the world can feel safe in their alliance with us?" The more relevant question should be with what ally can America feel .

U.S. Sending Disaster Team, Initial $1 Million To Nepal

(Adds Kerry statement, urban search and rescue team)

WASHINGTON, April 25 (Reuters) - The United States will send disaster response and rescue teams to Nepal and has authorized an initial $1 million in aid after a major earthquake killed hundreds in the mountainous Asian nation, U.S. Secretary of State John Kerry said on Saturday.

"We are working closely with the government of Nepal to provide assistance and support," he said in a statement.

The United States Agency for International Development (USAID) said in a tweet it was working with the Office of U.S. Foreign Disaster Assistance (OFDA) to launch a disaster response team and described the funding as an initial amount "to address immediate needs."

2015					MAY	
SUNDAY	MONDAY	TUESDAY	WEDNESDAY	THURSDAY	FRIDAY	SATURDAY
					1	2
3	4	5	6	7	8	9
10	11	12	13	14	15	16
17	18	19	20	21	22	23
24	25	26	27	28	29	30
31						

May is the offspring of the green tree........

BE CREATIVE.GO OUT AND DESIGN SOMETHING

Design & Concepts

Join our mailing list
and get a free 1
month Subscription
to our magazine!

Owner

Design & Concepts L.L.C
Elizabeth Chavez
770-765-0687
www.designandconcepts.biz
www.lisabethdesignmagazine.com

Creativedesignconcepts@rocketmail.com

Place orders by email or contact

BE CREATIVE.GO OUT AND DESIGN SOMETHING

Design & Concepts

House of Lisabeths Design Magazine
We were started in 2013 as an independent magazine. Our focus is fashion, health and business. We pride ourselves in the design and diversity we offer.
Exclusivity
Our focus is fashion , health and business. Our fashion section includes tips and trends from all over! We also have a online blog that gets tons of clicks per day, check us out online at ......
Our business section is used for local or national business to place a Ad or listing of them selfs. We have total exclusivity In that they connect with not only our magazine but all of our networks simultaneously.
Our hope is to reach across the world along with Water 4 Kids International. We plan to donate proceeds to this foundation. Our hope is to provide safe water for east Africa.
Check us out on line, Facebook, Twitter, Tumblr, Amazon, and our affiliates websites like Design & Concepts.

Get a 1 year subscription for $ 19.99——————— ☐

Personal Information

Name:_____   Email _____

Address_____, Phone _____

City, State, Zip _____

Payment Enclosed——————————- ☐
Pay Later——————————- ☐

Send To:

Design & Concepts

" Fill out above info and return to address given"
MIAMI
Liz Chavez
8369 NW 66 ST #3684
Miami, FL 33166

We also take check, cash and money orders.

Remember when you send for a subscription you get a free t-shirt that says "Lisabeth Design"

Thanks for supporting our fashion blog and Section!

Also with your subscription get a free Lisabeth Design T-Shirt

Available for Men and Women

Check out Design & Concepts Blog

I recognize that preaching the importance of social media to businesses is a little redundant. By now, buy-in to social media marketing is near ubiquitous, but I still find that many organizations have a difficult time quantifying the value they can achieve through the strategic use of social media.

While I certainly don't have a silver bullet response to help everyone understand the actual quantitative value of social media marketing, there are some incredibly compelling stats I'm going to share here to help you understand just how important social platforms can be to your business.

91% of people have gone into a store because of an online experience. (Source: Marketing Land)

This is a crazy statistic, but intuitively makes sense. Think about your own behaviour as a consumer. You probably spend a great deal of time researching the products and services you're interested in online before making a purchase decision. And why wouldn't you? With a world of information at your fingertips, it would be foolish to not research purchases online, read reviews, look up prices, get a sense for who you will be working with, determine how products are supported and serviced, and more.

Join the Cause!
Check out the " Design for Sick Kids Campaign'

Our Mission
In the beginning we wanted a way to show our passion for design.
But this project is turning to be more then that. With so many sick
kids and so much that we can give we thought about giving the gift
of design.

What We Need & What You Get
Here is what we need
1000 cards , either designed by you or who ever
A contribution as well to our campaign

The Impact
With every card made we will donate a dollar and that card to a local
hospital of our choice. So think about all the kids you can help by
creating there Christmas card or birthday card and also the contri-
butions that come with it.
Remember every card made we donate $ 1.00 to the cause
Also share your design with the people and get your picture taken
with the kids

Other Ways You Can Help Check out our websites
www.designandconcepts.net for more updates on more causes!

http://www.indiegogo.com/projects/design-a-card-for-your-kids/

Join the Cause!

Check out the "House Of Lisabeth Design Magazine- We are Here"

Our Mission
House of Lisabeth Design magazine is a new trendy magazine for fashion, trends, and business networking.

Hi, my name is Elizabeth Chavez I am the owner of Design & Concepts and am the editor and creator of " House of Lisabeth Design Magazine"

We are reaching out to you for a launch of our new magazine. For us it's important to get contributors from people who have faith in this magazine and want to help us launch it.

What were looking for is anything from 1 dollar to 100 dollars...The more people we reach the faster we will get to our goal.

Remember be creative go out and design something!

Also be sure to check us out on Facebook, Twitter, Amazon, Tumblr and our affiliate blogs , Lisabeth blog, and Design and Concepts blog

Also with your subscription get a free Lisabeth Design T-Shirt

Available for Men and Women

Design & Concepts Services

Www.designandconcepts.us

www.lisabethdesignmagazazine.com
www.lisabethfashionmagazine.us

Design & Concepts is an online service provider for design and advertising. We specialize in brochures logos and business cards as well as t shirts and sickies. We also do local advertising with in the community. Our prices vary with design but...

Our packages start at $55.00 per package!
Package includes : 200 prints
Gloss or matt finish is $10.00 per set/ per 200

Our Packages also include our Marketing Services, and Discounts on our Advertising Specials in our magazine, House of Lisabeth Design Magazine!

Also with your subscription get a free Lisabeth Design T- Shirt

Available for Men and Women

Design & Concepts Services:

Create various ads and place it on all social networks, web pages and create you tube videos to sell, demonstrate and promote your product

Also place your ad on any media source that is available We can take your campaign and place it on any other media resources you have available not just create a web presence awareness but really hit the market.

.We use digital media like

Email marketing, social network campaigns, print distribution, custom Web Design and SEO

Funny Definition of the month

Climate control[edit]

Climate control refers to the control of temperature and relative humidity for human comfort, health, and safety; for the technical requirements of machines and processes; and in buildings, vehicles, and other enclosed spaces.

Comfort[edit]

Humans are sensitive to humidity because the human body uses evaporative cooling, enabled by perspiration, as the primary mechanism to rid itself of waste heat. Perspiration evaporates from the skin more slowly under humid conditions than under arid conditions. Because humans perceive a low rate of heat transfer from the body to be equivalent to a higher air temperature,[2] the body experiences greater distress of waste heat burden at high humidity than at lower humidity, given equal temperatures.

For example, if the air temperature is 24 °C (75 °F) and the relative humidity is zero percent, then the air temperature feels like 21 °C (69 °F).[3] If the relative humidity is 100 percent at the same air temperature, then it feels like 27 °C (80 °F).[3] In other words, if the air is 24 °C (75 °F) and contains saturated water vapor, then the human body cools itself at the same rate as it would if it were 27 °C (80 °F) and dry.[3] The heat index and the hu-

WHY ADVERTISE WITH ....
HOUSE OF LISABETH DESIGN MAGAZINE
LISABETH FASHION MAGAZINE

Our reach is growing, Our audience is picking us up, and our target audience is you!

Looking for classifieds, if interested submit your business and information and well help you out!

Liz:

LIZKELLY12@OUTLOOK.COM

Meet The Editor And Owner…..

 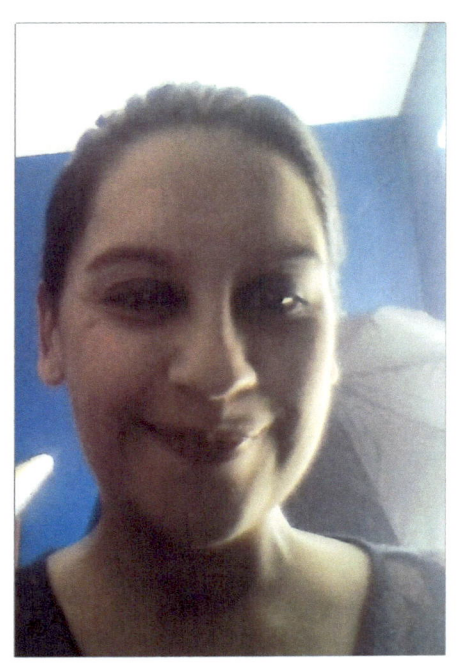

Elizabeth Chavez 28,,, Currently the owner of Design & Concepts LLC , and Editor of House of Lisabeth Design Magazine, and our newest Lisabeth Fashion Magazine. As an entrepreneur in her own field she manages both her business and love of de-signing in her everyday life. She works hard by involving all things that she can in many projects that she is involved with. One of her favorite is working on her fashion ideas blogging, posting or putting suggestions out all together.

Classifieds

F.O.B. SALES MANAGER
Harvest Sensations, LLC • Los Angeles, CA • 3/23/2015
Job Description
Harvest Sensations is a national fresh produce distributor and processor with state of the art and strategically located facilities in Miami, Florida and Los Angeles, California. We are looking for a dynamic, energetic and experienced FOB sales person.

http://www.careerbuilder.com/jobseeker/jobs/jobdetails.aspx?sc_cmp1=js_jrp_jobclick&APath=2.21.0.0.0&job_did=JHT4R870D5K1T0SCPTN&showNewJDP=yes&IPath=QHTV0A

Sports Minded: "Adversity causes some men to break; others to break records" Sales / Marketing / Entry Level!

-

Job Description

Account Executives primary role and responsibility is to create, develop, harness and execute strategic sales and marketing for our clients. Account executives will be trained and developed to use a proven system outlined to grow business relations assigned by the Managing Partner to whom they will directly report.

-

http://www.careerbuilder.com/jobseeker/jobs/jobdetails.aspx?sc_cmp1=js_jrp_jobclick&APath=2.21.0.0.0&job_did=JHS3CY73

Classifieds

Sales Consultants
Job Description

buybuyBABY in is seeking passionate, energized, customer-obsessed people who thrive on a fast pace, enjoy working in a team environment, and delight in making every customer experience remarkable.

http://www.careerbuilder.com/jobseeker/jobs/jobdetails.aspx?sc_cmp1=js_jrp_jobclick&APath=2.21.0.0.0&job_did=J3H4B563P2CFYBL25T2&showNewJDP=yes&IPath=QHTV0Q

Why Advertise with
House of Lisabeth Design Magazine
Lisabeth Fashion Magazine

Our reach is out there growing !!!!

www.ingramcontent.com/pod-product-compliance
Lightning Source LLC
Chambersburg PA
CBHW041513280526

45792CB00004B/1238